Conversations With The Savior

Dialogues And Children's Sermons For Lent And Easter

Donald H. Neidigk

CSS Publishing Company, Inc., Lima, Ohio

CONVERSATIONS WITH THE SAVIOR

Copyright © 2001 by
CSS Publishing Company, Inc.
Lima, Ohio

The original purchaser may photocopy material in this publication for use as it was intended (i.e., worship material for worship use; educational material for classroom use; dramatic material for staging or production). No additional permission is required from the publisher for such copying by the original purchaser. Inquiries should be addressed to: Permissions, CSS Publishing Company, Inc., P.O. Box 4503, Lima, Ohio 45802-4503.

Scripture quotations are from the *Holy Bible, New International Version*. Copyright © 1973, 1978, 1984 International Bible Society. Used by permission of Zondervan Bible Publishers. All rights reserved.

Library of Congress Cataloging-in-Publication Data

Neidigk, Donald, 1949-
    Conversations with the Savior : dialogues and children's sermons for Lent and Easter / Donald H. Neidigk.
       p. cm.
    ISBN 0-7880-1783-7 (pbk. : alk. paper)
    1. Lenten sermons. Dialogue sermons. 3. Children's sermons. 4. Bible. N.T. John—Sermons. 5. Sermons, Americans—20th century. I. Title.
BV4277 .N35 2001
252'.62—dc21
                                                                                00-046843
                                                                                     CIP

For more information about CSS Publishing Company resources, visit our website at www.csspub.com.

ISBN 0-7880-1783-7   PRINTED IN U.S.A.

*To my quiver full of blessings,
Matthew, Nathan, and Stephen*

(Psalm 127:4-5)

Table Of Contents

Preface   7

Ash Wednesday
   I Am The Bread Of Life   9
   Children's Sermon   14

Lent 1
   I Am   17
   Children's Sermon   23

Lent 2
   I Am The Gate   25
   Children's Sermon   31

Lent 3
   I Am The Good Shepherd   33
   Children's Sermon   38

Lent 4
   I Am The Resurrection And The Life   41
   Children's Sermon   47

Lent 5
   I Am The Way And The Truth And The Life   49
   Children's Sermon   54

Maundy Thursday
   I Am The True Vine   57
   Children's Sermon   62

Good Friday
    I Am He   65
    Children's Sermon   70

Easter Sunday
    I Am The Light Of The World   73
    Children's Sermon   78

Preface

Lent is a season that helps us draw closer to the Lord Jesus Christ into whose death, burial, and resurrection we have been baptized. It is a time of self-denial, of growth, and of good works motivated by the Holy Spirit working through the Word in the lives of those who name Jesus as Savior. It is a time to contemplate who Jesus is and what he does for us.

This Lenten series, *Conversations With The Savior,* was written to help God's people draw closer to Jesus through his many *I AM* statements in the Gospel of John. Though the dialogues are fictional, the message is scriptural. It is hoped that listeners may grow in faith and understanding as they find something of themselves in the characters who talk with Jesus.

Accompanying each conversation is a children's sermon that strives to reinforce the featured *I AM* statement. Easily obtained household items help tell the story. The pastor or any layperson can present the children's sermon. Two persons, in costume or not, are required to present the conversations. They may be as dramatic or as simple as local circumstances indicate.

Ash Wednesday
Exodus 15:9-15
John 6:25-35 (36-59)

I Am The Bread Of Life

BENJAMIN: I'm hungry, Jesus!

JESUS: Benjamin, how could you be hungry? You were there for the feast on the mountain, weren't you? You and 5,000 other men had all the bread and fish you could eat. There was plenty left over for another meal, and that was only yesterday. How could you be hungry?

BENJAMIN: How could I be hungry? Why, from trying to find you, of course! Just as we were about to crown you king after that great talk you gave and then the feast, you disappear! None of the Romans or the Herod family ever took care of us like you did, and from only five loaves of bread and two fish! What a candidate! But then you left in such a hurry. I had to run all the way around the sea of Galilee to find you again. Of course I'm hungry!

JESUS: So you're hungry again and you've come to me for more fish and bread, is that it? Benjamin, if I gave you fish and bread every day, you would still be hungry. It's not fish and bread that you need.

BENJAMIN: Oh, no, Jesus. I'm a man of simple needs. Bread and fish are all I want. And you're the man for the job. If I had other needs, I'm sure you could meet them too. I've seen you do it. I was there when the official at Cana asked you to heal his son. He begged you to come to his home. But you just said, "You may go. Your son will live." And at that very hour, the boy was healed. Then there was the healing of the paralyzed man at the miracle pool of Bethesda. No one cared enough to put him in the water. But you cared and simply said to him, "Pick up your mat and walk," and he did.

JESUS: Just as I thought. You don't really want me to be your king after all, do you?

BENJAMIN: Of course I do, Jesus! That's why I'm telling you all this. How could I say it more clearly? You give bread and fish to the hungry! You heal the sick! What else could a man ask for in a king?

JESUS: But that's not why I've come, Benjamin. Feeding the hungry and healing the sick are just signs pointing to something beyond themselves. I've come to satisfy a far greater hunger than your need for bread. I've come to heal a sickness far greater than any fever or palsy.

BENJAMIN: Good! Good! I'm interested! The day you fed all 5,000 of us men with only five loaves and two fish, I knew you were the man we needed. Why, you were just like Moses back in the days when he gave us manna in the wilderness, and taught us God's law. It's been such a long time since we've had a leader like him, but now you're here, giving us bread, teaching us. Where do I sign up?

JESUS: Benjamin, what I offer you is not manna, but True Bread from Heaven, and what I teach you is not law that condemns but Good News that forgives and brings eternal life. Are you not hungry, Benjamin, for God's forgiveness and the Bread of Life?

BENJAMIN: I ... I'm not sure I understand, Jesus.

JESUS: No, Benjamin, you don't understand, and you won't understand until you discern the nature of your true hunger and partake of the only Bread that can satisfy that hunger. Not long ago, I stopped at a well in Samaria. It was during the heat of the day. A woman came by herself to draw water. Do you know what kind of woman comes at noon to draw water by herself, avoiding the other women who come in the morning when it's cool? A sinful woman, Benjamin. I told her that if she would but ask, I would give her living water, water that would never leave her thirsty again. She begged me for this living water, but what she had in mind, Benjamin, was water that could be hers without the labor of coming to the well. She wanted only a cool stream by the door of her house. But even if she had such a stream, she would still be thirsty.

BENJAMIN: Still thirsty, even with cool, fresh water just outside her door? I don't think so.

JESUS: Oh yes, Benjamin. You see, it was not physical water that she needed. If her need were physical, she would have been satisfied long ago — married five times, living with a man who was not her husband. Benjamin, her thirst wasn't for ordinary water, but for peace with God, for forgiveness, for an abundant and eternal life that could be hers only by turning to the giver of life. Oceans of water and a thousand lovers could never meet that need.

BENJAMIN: You mean, Jesus, that it isn't bread and fish for my stomach and healing for my body that I need, but food and healing for my soul? Is that what you're trying to tell me?

JESUS: How could I make it more clear, Benjamin?

BENJAMIN: But, Jesus, the woman of which you speak is a Samaritan, and I'm a Jew, a descendant of Abraham, an heir to the covenant promises. And, Jesus, I've worked hard to keep God's commandments. I've not committed adultery as did that woman. I don't have her need of forgiveness.

JESUS: Benjamin, after the feast on the mountain, there was much bread and fish left that you and others took home. Did you share that abundance with the hungry in your village? And though you saw me heal the paralyzed man by the pool at Bethesda, did you visit your sick neighbor? Did you wash him? Feed him? Clean his house? And though you've never committed adultery, have you lusted? Have you always lived with your wife in kindness and understanding, seeking to meet her needs rather than demanding that she meet yours? And in your work, Benjamin, have you always given a hard day's work for your pay? Have you sought the well being and success of the one who hired you, or has your goal been your own success? I know you're not wealthy, Benjamin, but have you returned to God the first fruits of his provision for you, or have you indulged yourself and given him the leftovers? Benjamin, are you sure you have no need of forgiveness? Are you sure you only need another loaf of bread?

BENJAMIN: I have been a fool, Jesus. It's just as you say. I am no better than the woman at the well. You have read my heart, and what is written there shames me. A whole bakery could not satisfy the need of my soul for the Bread of Life. But tell me, Jesus, where can I find the Living Water and the Bread from Heaven that you speak of?

JESUS: I am the Bread of Life, Benjamin. I am the Bread of God who comes down from heaven and gives life to the world. He who comes to me will never go hungry and he who believes in me will never be thirsty.

BENJAMIN: Jesus, I'm beginning to understand. Let me follow you as you teach and heal that I might learn more.

JESUS: It is not to the towns and villages of Galilee that you must follow, Benjamin, but to the cross. The cross is why I've come. At the cross I give my life, my flesh, for the life of the world. There, for your sins, for the sins of the Samaritan woman, for the sins of all mankind, I give up myself to die. This is the bread of which I speak. If anyone eats this bread, my flesh sacrificed there, he will live forever.

BENJAMIN: How can this be, Jesus?

JESUS: By faith, Benjamin. He who comes to me in faith, believing that I am the Bread of Life, that my flesh is real food and my blood real drink, will never go hungry or be thirsty again. Whoever believes in me, whoever partakes of the Living Bread by faith, will have eternal life and be raised up at the Last Day.

BENJAMIN: But, Jesus, how can I follow you if you are dead? How can I believe in one who leaves me? How can I partake of the Bread of Life if the Bread is gone?

JESUS: I can see that you are truly hungry, Benjamin. A grave of death cannot hold the Bread of Life. Though I die, yet I will be raised up to bring you and all who believe life. Whoever believes and is baptized shares in my death and burial and life. Whoever prays, "Give us this day our daily bread," is fed not only with earthly bread, but the Bread from Heaven. Whoever partakes of my Holy Supper, enjoys a feast in which this prayer is answered unto eternal life.

BENJAMIN: I am far hungrier than I once thought, Lord Jesus. Give me this day, the daily bread of which you speak.

JESUS: I am the Bread of Life. He who feeds on this bread will live forever. He who comes to me will never go hungry. Welcome, Benjamin, to the feast of faith.

Prayer

Lord, we are hungry. We have tried to satisfy our hunger with possessions, with success, with sensuality, and with power. But it's never worked. We know our hunger really results from turning away from you, and that nothing can satisfy us but your Son, Jesus Christ, the Bread of Life. Grant that we come to him in faith. So fill us with his love and forgiveness that we might never be hungry again. In his name we pray. Amen.

Ash Wednesday
John 6:25-35

Children's Sermon

Item needed: bread, sliced or unsliced

Hello, boys and girls. I'm so happy to see so many of you here as we begin the Lenten season. Lent is a special time to grow in our love for Jesus and our neighbor. Part of growing in our love for Jesus is learning more about who he is.

Tonight I've brought a loaf of bread to help us learn. Do you like bread? So do I. Would you like a piece? (*Give each child a piece of bread.*) I bet some of you are hungry. Did all of you eat before you came? (*Listen to answers.*) Just as I thought, some of you came to church hungry.

But didn't you have lunch? If you had lunch, why are you hungry? (*Allow one or two children to speak.*) Right! Lunch was over seven hours ago. Ordinary food doesn't fill us up for long, does it? But guess what! There is food that can satisfy us forever.

It's Jesus. He calls himself the Bread of Life. That means that he meets our most important needs. When we sin we need forgiveness. When we die we need life. When we're sad we need joy. These are our greatest needs and only Jesus can satisfy them.

Do you believe in Jesus? Good, so do I. I'm so happy to be forgiven and loved by him. But did you know that many other people don't know Jesus is the Bread of Life? Let's pray that they will know him and that God will show us how to share the Good News of Jesus with others.

Prayer

Lord Jesus, thank you for being the Bread of Life. When we are unhappy or feeling guilty, help us know that only you can forgive us and bring us joy that lasts. Give us faith to trust you and courage to share your love with others. In your holy name we pray. Amen.

Lent 1
Genesis 12:1-7
John 8:(13-47) 48-58

I Am

REUBEN: Jesus, I know you've had a busy day, and I'm not one of your Twelve. But perhaps you'd have a moment for me anyway.

JESUS: What is it, Reuben?

REUBEN: You use my name! How is it that you know me, Jesus? I've watched you and listened to you from a distance, as one of the crowd, but we've never spoken. You already know me? That's the sort of thing that troubles me about you, Jesus.

JESUS: Yes, I know you, Reuben, and when you know who I am perhaps you won't be so troubled. But now you've come to me for a reason. Speak freely. I'll not condemn you.

REUBEN: That's part of it, right there, Jesus. The Pharisees condemn people like me. I'm a sinner, not much of a synagogue goer at all, and seldom at the feasts in Jerusalem. Yet you don't speak to people like me as the Pharisees do. This morning, when the teachers of the law and the Pharisees dragged that adulterous woman before you in the temple court, you didn't condemn her. Nor did you overrule the law of Moses. Everyone knew she was guilty but all you said was, "Whoever is without sin, let him cast the first stone." And all her accusers left, condemning themselves. But you forgave her. Why Jesus?

JESUS: Because she, like you, Reuben, was already crushed with a burden of guilt and shame. What she needed was not stones, but forgiveness.

REUBEN: And the others? What about them?

JESUS: Sadly, they remain in their sins. Until they see their true condition before God as sinful and shameful, every bit as wretched as that woman's condition, they will never seek nor will they find the forgiveness I offer.

REUBEN: And that's part of why I need to talk with you, too, Jesus. Who are you to offer forgiveness to sinners? Only God can forgive sins. When you healed that man lowered to you through the roof, and forgave his sins too, that really raised some eyebrows. "Who can forgive sins but God alone?" they were asking. Some think what you did borders on blasphemy.

JESUS: Reuben, I do only what my Father has sent me to do.

REUBEN: That's another thing everyone is talking about. Just who is your Father? Most people think Joseph, the carpenter, was your father. But what authority would that give you to forgive sins? Others say you have no legitimate father. They say you are a Samaritan, a half-breed, a teacher of lies.

JESUS: And what do you think, Reuben?

REUBEN: As yet I don't know what to think, Jesus. I'm not sure I even know what you mean by "Father."

JESUS: It is my Father who sent me and who bears witness of me. It is his works that I do and his words that I speak. I am not of this world, Reuben. Look at my works, listen to my words, and you'll know who my Father is.

REUBEN: It's that kind of talk that mystifies me, Jesus. I'm trying to understand you, but you speak in riddles. How will I ever know who you really are?

JESUS: I can see that still you don't know me. If you knew me, you would know my Father also. He sent me to bring you freedom, Reuben. Hold to my teaching, Reuben, and you'll know the truth about me and in that truth you'll be free.

REUBEN: Free? I can tell you know far more about me than I know about you, Jesus. It's bad enough to have these pagan Romans on every corner telling us what to do, and their tax collectors endlessly shaking us down for more than we owe. But worse is the never ending guilt I feel. I try to forget, but my sins haunt me, especially in the quiet of the night as I lie on my bed. My rabbi did his job well teaching me the Law. He would boast that he was a free son of Abraham. Perhaps *he* was, but thanks to him, I know *myself* to be a slave of sin. If I could only find this freedom of which you speak, Jesus.

JESUS: But, Reuben, if the Son sets you free, you shall be free indeed!

REUBEN: It's not just Romans and tax collectors and guilt that enslave me, Jesus. It's our own leaders. Not long ago, I visited the synagogue once again. I admit it had been a while. But those pompous wind-bags. You know how they are. Well, I went. You were even there that day. You healed that man with the withered hand. Remember? But because it was the Sabbath, they came after you like a pack of wolves! They teach that freedom is in the Law. Some freedom! Thank God you disregarded their law, restoring the man's hand, giving him the only freedom he'd had in years.

JESUS: It's not God's law that they're teaching, Reuben, but their own. If God's law were truly their concern, they would rejoice in a man made well. And if Abraham were really their father they would seek to protect a man's life. But already they are plotting to kill me. I forgive sinners and heal the sick and lame. Where is the crime in this? Who but the devil would stand in the way of freedom and forgiveness and healing and life?

REUBEN: That is what I wonder too, Jesus.

JESUS: They claim Abraham as their father, Reuben, but a child of Abraham has the faith and does works of Abraham. I speak the truth of God and they say I'm demon possessed. I forgive a sinful woman and heal a crippled man and they plot to kill me. Just who is it that is demon possessed, one who speaks truth and forgives and heals? Or is it one who denies the truth and plots murder? I know who *my* Father is, but *their* father is the devil.

REUBEN: Jesus, is your Father greater than our father Abraham?

JESUS: In faith, Abraham saw my day, and was glad. Reuben, before Abraham was, I Am.

REUBEN: You are speaking words too difficult for a simple man like me, Jesus. And when you speak that Name, you are using a word too holy for a sinner like me to mention. You are saying things spoken by God to Moses. I am afraid, Jesus!

JESUS: Reuben, in the beginning was the Word, and the Word was with God, and the Word was God. I am that Word.

REUBEN: Jesus, you'll have to help me. I just don't understand.

JESUS: In him was life, and the life was the light of men. The light shines in the darkness, but the darkness has not comprehended it.

REUBEN: Jesus, who are you?

JESUS: He was in the world, and though the world was made through him, the world did not recognize him.

REUBEN: Jesus, these mysteries are beyond me. You are speaking things of God that are too deep for me.

JESUS: The Word became flesh. He is with you even now, Reuben. You have seen his glory, the glory of the One and Only who came from the Father, full of grace and truth.

REUBEN: Flesh? Grace? Truth? I've seen all of these in you, Jesus. Are you really the One who bears that holy Name, the I Am, the one who spoke to Moses? Are you the One promised through Abraham, the One through whom the whole world would be blessed?

JESUS: If you believe that I Am he, you will live and not die. When you have lifted up the Son of Man, then you will know that I Am he. If you hold to my teaching, the truth will set you free. If any one keeps my word, he will never taste death. Reuben, my word is the truth.

REUBEN: Jesus, I am not holy like Moses or Abraham. If you are the I Am, how can I, a sinner, come to you? Surely, to be in the presence of God is to die!

JESUS: No, Reuben. I have come that you might have life.

REUBEN: You, the I Am, have come to give me life? Me, obscure, unworthy Reuben? If you knew me as well as you seem to, you would turn me away for sure.

JESUS: Whoever comes to me I will never drive away, Reuben. All who receive me, all who believe in my name, become the children of God. Just come, Reuben. You'll find no stones, just forgiveness and life.

REUBEN: Lord Jesus, I believe. Help my unbelief. Lord Jesus, just as I am, I come.

Prayer

Lord Jesus, eternal "I Am," we cannot understand how the unapproachable, invisible God can come to us in human form like ourselves, but with timid faith we do believe this is just what you have done. And Lord, we are painfully aware of our sinfulness. We are embarrassed by what our hearts reveal and what you already know. Yet you bid us come and promise never to drive us away. Thank you for your welcome, your forgiveness, your gift of life. In your holy name we pray. Amen.

Lent 1
John 8:48-58

Children's Sermon

Item needed: a rock, about six inches across

Welcome, children! It's good to see so many of you back again this week, and some new comers, too! During Lent this year we're learning more about who Jesus is. Once he said about himself, "Before Abraham was, I Am." Now that's a puzzling thing for him to say, isn't it?

I've brought a rock to help us understand what Jesus meant. Would you like to hold it? (*Pass the rock around among the children.*) It's just an ordinary rock, but I couldn't make a rock, could you?

How old do you think this rock is? (*Let children offer their guesses.*) Yes, it's thousands and thousands of years old. A lot older than you or I. How long ago do you think Abraham lived? Probably about 4,000 years ago. That's a long time, but it's still not very old compared to this rock.

Guess what? Jesus was alive before Abraham ever lived or this rock was even made. He said, "Before Abraham was, I Am." That means Jesus is forever. The Bible also says, "All things were made through him." Since all things, including rocks, were made through Jesus, who do you suppose he is? Yes, Jesus is God.

It makes me so happy to know that Jesus came to earth so that we could know God. By believing that Jesus is God who has come to save us, we have all our sins forgiven and a wonderful home in heaven.

This is a heavy and very old rock I'm holding, but someday it will turn to sand, but heaven won't turn to sand. Heaven is forever because Jesus is forever. Let's pray.

Prayer
    Lord Jesus, we are just children and don't understand how you can be God and a human being like us who can be born and live and die. But we know it's true becaue your word says so. Help us always believe that you are our God and Savior who always lives to forgive our sins and take us to heaven. Amen.

Lent 2
Genesis 28:10-17
John 10:1-10

I Am The Gate

ELIEZER: Do you mind if I walk with you, Jesus?

JESUS: Of course you may, Eliezer. Your face betrays the anguish of your soul. What's troubling you, my friend?

ELIEZER: Jesus, I'm trying to be a faithful child of God, but I'm worried that perhaps I'm not. You see, my rabbi has told the whole congregation that if anyone acknowledges you as the Christ, he'll be put out of the synagogue.

JESUS: And that worries you?

ELIEZER: Oh, yes, Jesus. All it would take is three men who accuse me of wrong, and I'd be cut off from the fellowship for a day. If I continued to believe in you, the whole assembly could cast me out and treat me worse than a leper. My friends and neighbors would avoid me. I could talk with no one. They would let me buy food, but I would have to eat my bread by myself. And when I die, they would throw rocks at my grave. I couldn't bear that, Jesus.

JESUS: Tell me, Eliezer, what makes you think I might be the Christ?

ELIEZER: It's what you said and did back there in Jerusalem.

JESUS: Such as?

ELIEZER: Such as what you said to the Pharisees and teachers of the Law. You said, "If the Son sets you free, you will be free indeed." And, "If anyone keeps my word, he will never taste death." They didn't like what you said, and because of them, I'm afraid to believe it. I'm not free Jesus, and I'm afraid to die.

JESUS: And what is it that enslaves you, Eliezer? The Pharisees were highly insulted when I implied they weren't free. But you aren't insulted. Why? You think yourself to be a slave?

ELIEZER: I know myself to be a slave, Jesus, to everything and everyone, it seems. I'm a slave to those unclean Romans, taking my donkey whenever they feel like it, forcing me to pay their damnable taxes. I'm a slave to the Pharisees and teachers of the Law and the Rabbis; they're always watching me, catching me in every slip of the tongue, in every offering I forget to make and vow I can't keep, and cursing me for it. And worst, I'm a slave to my conscience. I know what I'm supposed to do, and I just can't do it.

JESUS: Well, Eliezer, at least you're free for a moment. You needn't fear my cursing you. Out here in the countryside, there's not a Pharisee in sight, nothing out here but sheep and that old sheep pen. It's been here a long time. A simple structure, isn't it? Just a square pen made of rough stones piled one on top of the other. And look! There's just a hole in the wall for a gate.

ELIEZER: But what does that have to do with me?

JESUS: There's no door in this gate opening, Eliezer. Do you know why? Because the shepherd is the gate. At night he leads his sheep into the safety of the pen. Then he lies down right here and sleeps on the ground. The sheep stay in the pen until dawn when the shepherd leads them back out to pasture.

ELIEZER: It wouldn't be too hard to climb over the wall and just take a sheep or two.

JESUS: True, but one would have to be a thief and robber and not the shepherd to steal sheep. The shepherd's job is to protect the sheep. Sheep thieves kill and destroy and seek only their own well being.

ELIEZER: That sounds like the teachers of the Law and the Pharisees. They don't care at all about us. You heard them when you healed the blind man. He'd been blind since he was born. No one could help him. He used to lie at the temple gate and beg for alms. Except on the Sabbath he wasn't supposed to beg. That was working. But how was he supposed to get food any other way? The Pharisees used to watch, hoping they might catch someone giving him a coin on the Sabbath. I was afraid to give him anything. But you weren't, Jesus. You made mud and put it in his eyes, and when he washed, he could see! You gave him his freedom! I gave him nothing. I was afraid.

JESUS: I gave him freedom and the Pharisees gave him grief. Right, Eliezer? It grieves me that men can be so blind and so willfully enslaved. Even my disciples had no interest in the blind man but why he was blind, whether it was his sin or his parents' sin that caused it. And when he could see again, all the Pharisees could think about was that he was healed on the Sabbath. Did you notice how pathetic his parents were? There wasn't the slightest hint of joy that their son could see, so afraid were they of being put out of the synagogue. Oh, how they needed life and freedom and salvation!

ELIEZER: Those Pharisees and teachers of the Law have us trapped and enslaved by fear, Jesus. And there's no way out! If only there were some door, some gate out of this misery!

JESUS: I am the Gate.

ELIEZER: Jesus, you gave the woman taken in adultery her dignity and freedom back. You rescued her from those wolves. I wish I could be forgiven like her.

JESUS: I am the Gate!

ELIEZER: There was no one to help that poor cripple at the pool of Bethesda. The angel would stir the water but no one would put him in to be healed. But you spoke to him, Jesus. "Take up your mat and walk!" you said. And he did! At last he was whole and free! I'd like to be free and whole like him.

JESUS: *I am the Gate!*

ELIEZER: Jesus, I feel just like a sheep trapped in this pen about to be stolen by thieves and robbers and fed to the wolves, with no way out. In the synagogue school, I learned a Psalm of David. It said, "The Lord is my Shepherd, I shall not want. He makes me to lie down in green pastures. He leads me beside still waters. He restores my soul." That's what I would like to believe about the Lord, but that's not the Lord these teachers show me. Jesus, can't you see I've followed you all the way out here for some answers? Help me, Jesus!

JESUS: Eliezer, *I am the Gate.*

ELIEZER: You're the Gate, Jesus?

JESUS: I am the Gate. You're one of my sheep, Eliezer. The reason you've come out to me here in the countryside is because you've heard my voice and know me not to be a thief and robber like the others.

ELIEZER: You're the Gate, Jesus?

JESUS: You were mine even before you were born. It's you're name I'm calling, Eliezer, not for guilt, not for slavery, not for fear, but for salvation and life.

ELIEZER: Jesus, you're the Gate?

JESUS: Yes, I'm the Gate. Whoever enters through me will be saved. He will come in and go out and find pasture. I go before my sheep, facing danger, even dying for them, that they might never fear walking through the valley of the shadow of death.

ELIEZER: You mean, Jesus, that by believing in you, I'm not a slave anymore, to Roman or Pharisee or even my guilty conscience? You mean, Jesus, that it's not just the sinful woman you forgive, but me? And it's not just a cripple by the pool that you make whole, but me? And it's not just the physically blind but the blind in heart that you make see, spiritually blind sinners like me?

JESUS: I am the Gate.

ELIEZER: But I have nothing to offer you Jesus, nothing with which to pay for these treasures.

JESUS: It's not the sheep's job to care for the shepherd, but the shepherd for the sheep. Enter through me and be saved. Come in and go out through me and find pasture. I have come that you might have life, and have it abundantly. Life is God's free gift to you, Eliezer. I am the Gate.

ELIEZER: How can I be sure, Jesus?

JESUS: Your own words have already spoken what you have heard and seen; sins forgiven, blindness restored, freedom gained. You have heard my voice and have come. Eliezer, you know I am the Gate.

ELIEZER: Yes, Jesus. I believe you are the Gate.

Prayer
Dear Lord Jesus, we have so many troubles that threaten to enslave us, worries about what others will think of us if we follow you, guilt that quenches our joy, sorrow in the travails of this world.

Open our ears that we might hear you calling us out of this slavery. Lead us through the gate that is you. Help us know that by faith in you, we are forgiven, we are free, and life is ours in abundance. In your name we pray. Amen.

Lent 2
John 10:1-10

Children's Sermon

Item needed: doorknob or gate latch

Well, hello! What a great group of children. I'm so glad you're here each week to learn more about who Jesus is. In the Gospel Lesson we read tonight, Jesus says, "I am the Gate." Some Bibles have, "I am the Door." But gates and doors are really the same, aren't they?

This is what I've brought to show you. (*Hold out the door knob or gate latch for all to see.*) Do you know what it is? (*Let children identify it.*) Yes, it's a door knob assembly, probably just like the one on your bedroom door.

Why do you suppose our houses have doors and door knobs and gates and gate latches? (*Allow several to answer.*) Of course, to keep our houses and yards safe. At night we lock the doors and gates. In the daytime we go in and out through them. If we want to go to school or the store, we go through the door first.

Jesus is like a door or gate. When we believe in Jesus as our Savior, we are going through a special door. On the other side of the door we find forgiveness of all our sins, all the bad things we do. We also find food and water, good things from God's word to make us strong in our faith.

If Jesus were not like a door, our sins would not be forgiven, and we would have no home in heaven. We'd always be in danger from the devil. But, praise God, Jesus is our Door. Let's thank God that he has given us a door to heaven in Jesus.

Prayer

Dear Lord Jesus, thank you for being our Door and Gate. When we hide behind you as our Door, you protect us from everything evil. Going through you by faith, all our sins are forgiven, you give us a home in heaven, and we are safe forever. For this we praise you, Lord. In your name we pray. Amen.

Lent 3
John 10:11-18
Ezekiel 34:1-10

I Am The Good Shepherd

JESUS: Ephraim, friend, where are you headed in such a hurry? It's much too hot for running! Just look at you, coughing, panting, about to stumble on the rocks. Surely you can spare a moment to catch your breath.

EPHRAIM: You know who I am? I was hoping that this wilderness was far enough from town that no one would recognize me. Is there no place I can go and be left alone?

JESUS: There's no need to run from me, Ephraim. I'll not harm you.

EPHRAIM: Say, I know you! You're the teacher from Galilee, the one they call Jesus!

JESUS: Yes, I'm Jesus.

EPHRAIM: Well, I haven't much use for religion. So if you'll excuse me, I'll be on my way.

JESUS: So that's why you're running. You're turning your back on God, is that it?

EPHRAIM: I suppose you could say that. I simply can't meet his demands and I'm tired of pretending I can. He tells me, "Walk before me and be blameless." Me, blameless? Have you read the Ten Commandments lately, Jesus? They look simple enough, but try keeping them. I have, and I've failed.

JESUS: The Pharisees don't think it's all that difficult.

EPHRAIM: That's because they think keeping the Law is all a matter of behavior. But thanks to you, Jesus, I've learned that keeping the Law is a matter of the heart too. I was there when you gave the Sermon on the Mount. To be angry with your brother is to be subject to judgment, you said. To lust after a woman is to commit adultery. Well, Jesus, I've been angry with my brother plenty of times, and my thoughts have often strayed in the presence of a beautiful woman. I'm guilty, and there's no denying it.

JESUS: What you need, Ephraim, is a Savior.

EPHRAIM: A Savior? And who might that be?

JESUS: The Good Shepherd.

EPHRAIM: Talk plainly, Jesus. I know nothing of Good Shepherds. But I do know about bad shepherds. Our people are sick to death of them. We've had kings who have gotten us into senseless wars and taxed us into poverty. We've had false prophets who have led us into immorality and paganism. We've had priests who have demanded sacrificial lambs for God but who have kept the choicest cuts for themselves. We've had Pharisees who have forced us to tithe everything but who would let their own parents starve. Show me this Good Shepherd, Jesus.

JESUS: The Good Shepherd bears no resemblance to the shepherds of Israel you've described, Ephraim. Those evil shepherds murder their sheep; the Good Shepherd lays down his life for his sheep. They drive their sheep to destruction with the rod; the Good Shepherd leads his sheep, guiding them with his staff, defending them with his rod. They endanger their sheep; the Good Shepherd puts his sheep behind him, and faces danger for them.

EPHRAIM: I've never met such a shepherd.

JESUS: Oh, but you have, Ephraim. The Good Shepherd knows you by name and calls you to follow him right now.

EPHRAIM: If I were to meet this Good Shepherd, surely he would send me away as soon as he learned of the many times I've sinned against God and my neighbor. I'm not the kind of sheep he'd want in his flock. That's why I'm running from God, Jesus. It's not just Israel's shepherds who have disappointed God. So have I.

JESUS: You are right, Ephraim. Both the leaders and the sheep have wandered from the Good Shepherd's fold. All of God's sheep have gone astray. Each has turned to his own way. But the Lord lays on the Good Shepherd the sin of them all.

EPHRAIM: That couldn't possibly apply to my sin, Jesus. If you only knew what I know about myself. I have so many secrets.

JESUS: Ephraim, I know far more about you than you could possibly imagine. The darkest secret of your soul is borne away by the Good Shepherd. For your transgressions he is pierced; crushed for your iniquities.

EPHRAIM: You mean there's hope for a runaway sheep like me, Jesus? Surely there are some better sheep than I that wouldn't require nearly as much attention or suffering.

JESUS: Ephraim, though 99 sheep were safe in the Good Shepherd's fold, and only one were to slip away, still the Good Shepherd would leave the 99 and find that one lost sheep. Nothing gives him or his Father or all the angels in heaven greater joy than one lost sheep that is found and brought home.

EPHRAIM: I think I'm the exception, Jesus. My needs are so great, there is no Shepherd who could supply them all. And besides, who am I to ever meet this Good Shepherd?

JESUS: Ephraim, I am the Good Shepherd; you shall never be in want.

EPHRAIM: You are the Good Shepherd, the one who lays down his life for the sheep? The one who bears my sin?

JESUS: I am he.

EPHRAIM: Jesus, I don't even have a home any more. I've embarrassed and shamed my family. The desert is my home, a place fit only for robbers and dangerous beasts.

JESUS: I am the Good Shepherd; I will make you lie down in green pastures.

EPHRAIM: I've been cut off from any refreshment, even a cup of water. And I deserve no better.

JESUS: I am the Good Shepherd; I will lead you beside quiet waters.

EPHRAIM: I've been given chance after chance to amend my sinful life and I've failed. My spirit within me is broken.

JESUS: I am the Good Shepherd; I will restore your soul.

EPHRAIM: I'm afraid to face death, especially with this burdened conscience that troubles me so. Soon I'll meet God, and then what?

JESUS: Don't be afraid, Ephraim. I am the Good Shepherd; though you walk through the valley of the shadow of death, I'll be with you, because I will have gone there before you.

EPHRAIM: But my enemies — temptation, the devil, the world — all these attack my soul and mind. Often I don't know which way to turn.

JESUS: I am the Good Shepherd; my rod, the rough timbers of my cross, will drive away every enemy; my staff, my word that I give you, will lead you along the right path.

EPHRAIM: Forgive me, Jesus, but how can I be sure? What token, what pledge do you give me that I can cling to? If you are to die for me, if you bear my sins on the cross, what assurance do I have that you are still with me, that your word is true?

JESUS: I am the Good Shepherd; I prepare for you a table of bread and wine, my body and blood, that you might always know of my victory over your enemies.

EPHRAIM: Then, Jesus, if all this is true, I have no need to run any more. Every good thing I need, especially mercy, is mine as a sheep of your flock. But Jesus, what if after coming to you I stray? I'm so prone to wandering off.

JESUS: My sheep listen to my voice. I know them, and they follow me. I give them eternal life and they shall never perish; no one can snatch them out of my hand.

Prayer
   Jesus, Good Shepherd, we've often wandered from your care, thinking perhaps another pasture was greener. But when we did, we found only desolation and sorrow. By your powerful word, always call us back to you that we might experience each day your overflowing cup of love and forgiveness. And thus, Lord, grant us the assurance that we will dwell in your house forever. Amen.

Lent 3
John 10:11-18
Psalm 23

Children's Sermon

Items needed: a heavy stick and a crooked shepherd's staff or cane

Hello and welcome! I'm so happy to see you all again. Today we're learning that Jesus is the Good Shepherd. Have you seen a picture of Jesus carrying a lamb? Who do you think the lamb is? (*Pause for responses.*) Yes, you and I are Jesus' lambs, and he is our shepherd. He leads us and carries us and protects us.

One of my favorite chapters in the Bible is Psalm 23. It starts out, "The Lord is my shepherd." It also says, "Your rod and your staff, they comfort me." I brought a shepherd's rod and staff to show you.

Would you like to hold my rod? (*Pass it around among the children.*) What's it like? Yes, it's short and heavy. What could you do with it? (*Allow children's suggestions.*) Right. We could use it to fight off a dangerous person or wild animal. Would a shepherd use this to hurt his sheep? No! He would protect his sheep with it, not hurt them.

Now look at my shepherd's staff. Why do you suppose it has a big hook on the end? (*Allow answers.*) Yes, so the shepherd can grab a sheep with it. If a sheep wanders off, or falls down in a hole, the shepherd can use his staff to bring it back or pull it out.

Jesus, our Good Shepherd, doesn't really have a rod or staff like these. He has something better. His rod is the cross. When Jesus died on the cross, he drove away all our enemies — sin and death and the devil. And Jesus' staff is his word. By believing his promises, Jesus keeps us safe in his flock and leads us to our home in heaven.

Prayer

Good Shepherd, thank you for going before us. Not only do you lead us, but you lay down your life to save us from sin. With the rod of your cross and the staff of your word, we are safe from every evil. Because of your love, we are not afraid. In your name we pray. Amen.

Lent 4
Job 19:23-27
John 11:17-27 (28-44)

I Am The Resurrection And The Life

DAN: Jesus, I'm angry with you.

JESUS: Oh, it's you, Dan. How did you find me, here in Ephraim, so far from Bethany?

DAN: I followed you here after you raised Lazarus from the dead.

JESUS: So you're angry. Now why could that be? You're not a teacher of the Law or priest, one of my usual enemies, so there's no danger you'll lose your job by believing in me. You're not a Roman, so you needn't fear I'll cause a riot and give you trouble. What's bothering you, Dan?

DAN: You already know what's bothering me, Jesus. Whatever I think or speak, you seem to know even before I do. It's about my brother.

JESUS: The one who died last year of that terrible fever; yes, I know. My heart grieves with you and your family. I've wept much because of your loss.

DAN: Have you, Jesus, really? I wish I could believe that. If you grieve as I do, why didn't you heal my brother? You have healed others. When I heard that you healed that royal official's son in Capernaum, I knew you had to be the Messiah. From that moment, I've been your disciple. I was there at the pool of Bethesda when you asked the crippled man if he wanted to get well. When he answered, "Yes," you said, "Get up! Pick up your mat and walk!" and he did.

JESUS: And this makes you angry, that two suffering souls are cured, and restored to those who love them?

DAN: Oh, no, Jesus. That's not what angers me. What angers me is that if you could heal them, you could have healed my brother. But you didn't. I prayed and prayed, but he just got weaker and weaker. Just a few weeks before you raised Lazarus from the dead, my brother died, but you never came.

JESUS: So that's it. You think I'm unfair. You think that I love others more than you and your family?

DAN: Yes, Jesus, that's what I think. And when you came all the way from across the Jordan to Bethany at the request of Martha and Mary when Lazarus died, I was sure of it. You wept with them, but not me. You went to Lazarus' tomb, but not my brother's. You restored Lazarus to his family, but my brother is still dead. I'm angry, Jesus.

JESUS: Believe me, Dan, when I say, I understand your anger. At the tomb of Lazarus where I wept, I was just as angry as you, even more. I was angry that Satan rejoices in grief and suffering and seeks to destroy faith just when it is most needed and yet most fragile. I was angry that sin has so wounded the whole human race that all must hurt and die. I was angry that self righteous men would do everything in their power to keep sinners from repenting and turning to me in faith.

DAN: You were angry, too, Jesus?

JESUS: Yes, Dan.

DAN: Then why haven't you stopped all these enemies of life and soul? Why haven't you healed all the sick and raised all the dead? And forgive me for being so selfish, Jesus, but why didn't you do these things for my brother?

JESUS: Dan, your brother's illness and death are a symptom of a far greater tragedy. He and all humankind are locked in a cycle of sin and death and suffering that would never end unless God intervened. And he has. He has sent me.

DAN: A few healings and two men raised from the dead — the widow's son and Lazarus — haven't done much to solve the problem, Jesus. I thought that when Messiah came, all the blind would see and all the lame would walk. I thought no one would ever die young again. The prophet Isaiah told us that in that wonderful day all of God's people would live out their years in peace, enjoying the fruits of their labor, surrounded by their children and grandchildren.

JESUS: Indeed they will! And blessings even far greater than these are in store for those who believe. But the weapons Messiah must wield to accomplish these things are far different from what most people expect. Dan, if I spent every hour of every day healing the sick and raising the dead, I would still not accomplish my mission. Sickness and death and grief would go on and on. Already, those whom I have healed are getting sick again, and soon the widow's son and even Lazarus will die once more. It is not a temporary healing or resurrection that they and your brother need, but an eternal one.

DAN: I don't understand, Jesus.

JESUS: The power of Satan must be broken, Dan, before a new heaven and a new earth without death and mourning and crying and pain can come to pass.

DAN: What can only one person — you, Jesus — do to break Satan's power? If we could see him, we could take up swords and spears and follow you into battle. But what are swords and spears against a fallen angel? They are nothing against such an enemy.

JESUS: You are right, Dan. Swords and spears will never defeat Satan. Indeed, they only help him. A different weapon is needed, a weapon despised and reviled by Jew and Gentile alike, an object of contempt in the world, but nonetheless, the most powerful weapon in the arsenal of God.

DAN: What is this weapon, Jesus?

JESUS: It is the cross. God has sent me to die on the cross, taking upon myself the sin and guilt of all mankind, dying in every sinner's place that Satan might no more have power over them, the power to accuse and condemn. I am to be pierced for every transgression, punished that you and the whole human race might have peace and be healed.

DAN: You would do this for me, for my brother, for others? Why, Jesus?

JESUS: Because God so loves the whole world that he has given me to die for you.

DAN: But how will your death solve anything, Jesus? If you are dead than the devil will have won.

JESUS: You are a good theologian, Dan. If I were to remain dead, then Satan will have won and there would be no hope for those who suffer and die. But death cannot hold me. On the third day, I will live. That is why I told Martha, the sister of Lazarus, "I am the Resurrection and the Life. He who believes in me will live, even though he dies."

DAN: So that's it! Because you die and rise again, my brother's death is temporary. And all our suffering is temporary. Though we grieve now, it won't be for long. Someday there'll be a whole new world full of life and beauty and laughter with no devil and no death.

JESUS: Yes, Dan.

DAN: And those will be days that will never end, as even the best of days do now. I'm beginning to understand, Jesus. Even if I had my brother back right now, and we were to celebrate with a great banquet, soon it would be over. It might be me who would get sick and die, or perhaps my mother. And grief would be with us all over again. But because of your death and rising again on the third day, the cycle is broken. Our suffering and grief are only for a little while. Oh, Jesus, I do understand, and I do believe you.

JESUS: Then you are not angry anymore, Dan?

DAN: No, Jesus, I'm not angry. Well, perhaps I am angry, but now I understand what you've come to do, and it helps me with my anger. When I think of that wonderful world without end that you've come to bring, my anger and grief somehow become bearable.

JESUS: Dan, your present suffering is real, and I feel it just as surely as if your brother's death were my own brother's death. But believe this: whatever our present suffering, it is not even comparable to the glory that is still to come.

DAN: Oh, what a happy day that will be! How I wish others could come to know the peace and happiness I suddenly feel, Jesus. Oh, how I wish they could know you as the Resurrection and the Life.

JESUS: So do I, Dan. So do I.

Prayer

Gracious God, we confess that we sometimes think you are unfair when the precious people we love are hurting. We have prayed in faith and with tears, yet sometimes the sick have not gotten well. When those we care about die, we wonder if you love us. Help us know that you do love us and hear our prayers. Help us believe that the greatest and most perfect answer to all our prayers is your own son, Jesus Christ, who has died to deliver us from sin and suffering and death. Thank you for the eternal life he has won for us. This we pray in the name of Jesus who is the Resurrection and the Life. Amen.

Lent 4
John 11:17-27

Children's Sermon

Item needed: an obituary page from the newspaper

Hi, children! Welcome back. Do you know what special day is coming soon? (*Answers will vary: birthdays, Mother's Day, Easter.*) The special day I have in mind is Easter. That's the day we celebrate Jesus' resurrection.

Does anyone know what an obituary is? (*Perhaps a child will know.*) An obituary is an announcement of someone's death in the newspaper. Families want all their friends and relatives to know when someone dies so everyone who wants to can come to the funeral or send a sympathy card.

Funerals are very sad events. When someone we love dies it makes us cry because we miss the person so much. Jesus visited his friends Martha and Mary when their brother Lazarus died. Jesus was just as sad as they were. Jesus cried.

But Jesus said, "I am the Resurrection and the Life. He who believes in me will live even though he dies." To show how much he loves us and how true his promise is, Jesus raised Lazarus to life again. He stood outside Lazarus' tomb and said, "Lazarus, come out!" And Lazarus did come out, alive once more.

But someday, Lazarus would die again, just as all of us will die. But Jesus changed things so that we don't have to be afraid. Jesus died for us and then rose from the dead on Easter morning. All who believe that Jesus died and rose for them will come to life someday and live forever with him. Won't that be a happy day!

Because Jesus gives new life to us all, we don't have to be afraid of dying. We still miss our loved ones who have died. But our sadness is turned to happiness when we remember that Jesus is the Resurrection and the Life.

Prayer

Loving God, thank you that Jesus died and rose again. Help us remember that because he lives, we do not have to be afraid of death. Give us faith that all who die, believing in Jesus, will someday rise to life never to die or hurt again. And Lord, as we trust you, fill our hearts with joy. In Jesus' name. Amen.

Lent 5
Isaiah 55:6-13
John 14:1-7 (8-14)

I Am The Way And The Truth And The Life

THOMAS: The Passover meal has ended, Jesus, and all Jerusalem is sleeping except for us. Shouldn't we return to the upper room so kindly offered us and spend the remainder of the night there?

JESUS: Thomas, I am going away, as I told you during the supper. I must prepare for my journey.

THOMAS: But surely, Jesus, the preparations will be much easier if you are rested. I am just one of your disciples but if the others are like me, we are all very tired.

JESUS: My enemies do not rest. Even now they too are preparing for my departure. I must prepare too.

THOMAS: How can you prepare when the few things you own are still in Bethany, and our feet are taking us to Gethsemane? What can be done in a garden at this late hour?

JESUS: I need nothing for my journey but the assurance of my Father's word in prayer.

THOMAS: Jesus, you keep speaking of your departure, of your going away. Over and over at the supper you spoke this way. You said we could not go with you. Yet we have gone everywhere else with you, for three years and more. Why not this time? Are you abandoning us, Jesus?

JESUS: No, Thomas. It is true that I am going away, but I would never abandon you. When I am gone, my Father will send the Holy Spirit. He will comfort and help you and be with you forever.

THOMAS: Jesus, forgive me, but what you say isn't making sense to me. You say you are going away and we cannot come, but you won't abandon us? In the upper room you said we couldn't follow you just now, but later we would. Jesus, just where are you going? And if we are to follow later, how do we find the way?

JESUS: Thomas, I am the Way and the Truth and the Life. No one comes to the Father except through me.

THOMAS: You are on your way to the Father, Jesus?

JESUS: Yes, Thomas.

THOMAS: You speak of the Father so often, Jesus, but who is the Father? Where is he?

JESUS: I and the Father are one.

THOMAS: Now I really don't understand, Jesus. We have confessed you as the Christ, the Son of God. But how can the Father be the Son too?

JESUS: I am always the Son and he is always my Father, yet we are one. And the Spirit whom Father and Son send after my departure is one with us.

THOMAS: Jesus, if you would show us the Father, we could understand.

JESUS: That is just what I have done, Thomas. He who has seen me has seen the Father. The words I speak are the Father's words. The works I do are the Father's works. Hear these words and see these works in faith, and in truth you will know the Father.

THOMAS: Then why must you go away, Jesus? If we know the Father through all that we hear and see in you, wouldn't it be better if you stayed?

JESUS: I am going to prepare a place for you, Thomas, a mansion of many rooms.

THOMAS: A mansion? If you would let me come now, I could help you build it, Jesus! And so could the others. Most of us are just fishermen, but with a master carpenter like you showing us how, we could do the work in no time! And we'd never have to be apart!

JESUS: I must build the mansion by myself, Thomas. You cannot help me. Though the mansion has room for all, the Father has called me to build it alone. With two beams and three nails, I will build this mansion.

THOMAS: Just two beams and three nails? Forgive me for doubting you, Jesus, but no mansion was ever built with just two beams and three nails. What shelter could that give? Who would want to live in it?

JESUS: Thomas, the two beams and the three nails are my cross. All who come to my cross in faith will enter the beautiful mansion I prepare for them. All who would come to the Father must come through the cross, for there is no other way.

THOMAS: So that's it. You're not going away as one would take a journey to Cyprus or Rome. You are going away in the sense of death. And that on a cross! Oh, Jesus, there has to be another way. It's just too shameful, too horrible.

JESUS: For the world, yes. For all who cling to this cross, no. This is the way to the Father and his mansion. By my death on the cross, you and all who believe will have a home in heaven forever. No one comes to the Father except through me.

THOMAS: No one comes to the Father except through you, Jesus? But the cross is much too offensive. Others will surely claim there are many ways. Just as it is said that all roads lead to Rome, surely there are other roads to the Father and his mansion.

JESUS: Do you know what you are saying, Thomas? All have sinned and so no one is worthy of a home in this mansion. That means that for everyone, entrance to the mansion is by God's grace. And if by grace, who is anyone to complain about a gracious gift? And, Thomas, if there are many ways, then the Father has sent his Son to die on the cross for nothing. To sacrifice his Son when there are other ways would make him a monster.

THOMAS: I mean no offense, Jesus. But still, some will say it's not fair. What of the multitudes of people who with great sincerity seek another way?

JESUS: Fairness is when one gets what he deserves. Remember the woman who was caught in adultery, in the very act? The religious leaders demanded that she be stoned to death. She had, after all, broken the Law of God. I never disagreed. But do you remember what I told her accusers, Thomas?

THOMAS: Yes, I do, Jesus. You said, "Whoever is without sin, let him cast the first stone."

JESUS: And then what happened?

THOMAS: All her accusers left.

JESUS: Why do you suppose that was?

THOMAS: Because they had all sinned and deserved the same punishment.

JESUS: Yes, Thomas. They all had sinned and deserved death. If entrance to my Father's house were based on sincere attempts to live righteously, no one would enter since all are sinners. That's what would be fair. But entrance into my Father's house isn't based on fairness, Thomas. It is based on my Father's grace. And in grace he has provided a way, my death on the cross. Would you rather have fairness or grace, Thomas?

THOMAS: I would rather you not have to die, Jesus. But if you must, then let me die with you that I might enter this mansion now and not have to wait.

JESUS: Thomas, you cannot come now. Someday you will, but for now, you must remain and tell others of my love and death for them that they might have life and a home in the mansion.

THOMAS: What if they won't believe? It's so hard even for me to accept. How will I know this is true?

JESUS: You have heard my words. You have seen my works. After my death on the cross, I will come to you again in person. Then you will know that I am the Way and the Truth and the Life.

THOMAS: Jesus, I'm so tired. Can we talk more about this tomorrow?

JESUS: No, Thomas, not tomorrow. But in three days we will.

Prayer

Lord Jesus, you have shown us the Father through your words and works of love. Though we are unworthy because of our many sins, nevertheless, you have prepared a way for us to enter the heavenly mansion through your cross. Help us never to be ashamed of it, but always recognize it as the only way of salvation. And send us the Spirit you have promised that we might not be alone but daily have power to believe and boldness to confess you as Savior. In your name we pray. Amen.

Lent 5
John 14:1-7 (8-14)

Children's Sermon

Item needed: a road map or an atlas

It's good to see you all again, children. It's getting closer and closer to Easter. Are you getting excited? I am too. Because Jesus came and died for our sins, and rose again on Easter Sunday, we have a way to heaven. Without Jesus, we would be lost and never find the way.

I brought my road atlas with me. Do you have one? When do your parents use a road atlas or map? (*Allow a child or two to answer.*) Yes, we use the atlas when we take a trip. The lines on the map are roads. Each road has a route number written by it. To get where we want to go, we find out where we are and then locate the place we want to go. Next we learn what road will take us there.

If you want to take a trip to Denver from Albuquerque, will the road to Phoenix get you there? No! Why not? (*Wait for answers.*) Right. Phoenix is southwest and Denver is north. We could drive for a long time on the road to Phoenix and never get to Denver. What road would we have to take? (*Let children look at the map.*) Yes, we would have to take this road and go north on it. It's called I-25.

How many of you would like to go to heaven someday and be with God? (*Children will raise their hands.*) Good! So do I. Some people think there are many roads to heaven. But did you hear what Jesus said in the Gospel Lesson? He said, "I am the Way, the Truth, and the Life. No one comes to the Father except through me."

That means only Jesus is the way to heaven. All who believe that he is God's Son who died for our sins on the cross and rose from the dead will live forever with God in heaven. I'm so happy that Jesus is the way to heaven, aren't you? Let's say, "Thank you," to God for Jesus.

Prayer

Dear Lord, thank you that you have sent your son Jesus to be our Savior. Without him, we would have no way to heaven. We would never see our heavenly Father. But you love us and sent Jesus so that all who believe in him might know the way to heaven. Help us show others that Jesus is the Way. In his name we pray. Amen.

Maundy Thursday
Galatians 5:16-25
John 15:1-17 1-9

I Am The True Vine

JESUS: John, my true and good friend! One last time we walk past the vineyard and climb the hill to the Garden of Gethsemane together.

JOHN: One last time, Jesus? We'll not be together after this?

JESUS: Not for a while, John.

JOHN: There's a change coming in the weather. I wonder how a storm will affect this vineyard?

JESUS: A vineyard! What a good picture of my relationship with you and the others.

JOHN: I'm not sure I understand, Jesus.

JESUS: Just see how the owner has worked hard getting this vineyard ready for spring. The walls around the field are all repaired. The dry weeds and debris of winter have been cleaned out. Look here! See how carefully the laborers have pruned each vine to promote an abundant crop of sweet grapes.

JOHN: They've done good work. It's almost as if the work were done lovingly.

JESUS: Yes, very lovingly, as has been my work with you and the rest of my disciples.

JOHN: This vineyard should yield a good crop at harvest time.

JESUS: With the right weather and care, a very good crop, just as I expect from you.

JOHN: A crop of grapes from me, Jesus? Do you want me to become a grape farmer?

JESUS: In a manner of speaking, yes. But not ordinary grapes, spiritual grapes.

JOHN: Spiritual grapes? How, Jesus?

JESUS: Remain in me, John, and you will bear fruit, much fruit.

JOHN: Just what is this spiritual fruit you speak of? What must I do to bear it? Are you sure I'm the right person? Whatever this spiritual fruit is, all too often my life seems more like a weed patch than a vineyard.

JESUS: It's not your doing at all, John. Do you remember how Isaiah the prophet speaks of God's vineyard?

JOHN: Yes, I do. As I recall, Isaiah's words aren't too comforting. God planted Israel as his vineyard hoping for a crop of justice and righteousness, but all he got were sour grapes. So he destroyed the vineyard, first by Assyria and Babylon and now by Rome. If it's up to me to bear fruit, I might bear sour grapes too, and then what?

JESUS: Go back to the beginning of the story, John. It was God who planted the vine. All that was necessary to bear fruit was for Israel to continue in faith.

JOHN: Faith, Jesus? That's all?

JESUS: Yes, John, faith. That's where Israel failed. They wanted another god, so finally God gave in to their demands. He let them go their own way, and that way led to Babylon. Now the Father has sent me to be the True Vine. He has sent me to succeed where

Israel failed. By faith in the Son, all who believe become branches on the vine who bear fruit.

JOHN: But what if I bear only a little fruit, Jesus?

JESUS: It's my Father's will that you bear much fruit. And you will! Just remain in the vine, John. I'll prune you and clean out all that keeps the fruit from growing. Through my word I'll cut away those influences in your life that would hinder your fruit bearing. Through the sufferings and trials you go through, my word will so strengthen your faith that your basket will overflow with fruit!

JOHN: What is this fruit, Jesus?

JESUS: All that you see in me, John: love for the unlovable, joy even in the troubles of life, peace in the midst of turmoil, patience even when pressed to the limit. All these, John, and more: kindness, goodness, gentleness, self-control.

JOHN: Yes, those are the qualities I see in you, Jesus. But when I get around others, I often don't see this fruit in myself. There's that Thomas who's so pessimistic, always expecting the worse. There's Peter, bragging about his faith one moment, and then speaking like a fool and an unbeliever the next. And there's our strange friend Judas, the greedy one. I don't trust that look in his eye. Oh, he's a hard one to love. My fruit basket still has lots of room in it, Jesus.

JESUS: That's all true, my friend. But the basket isn't for you to fill up alone. All of you together grow fruit for the basket. The vine has many branches. One may excel in patience, another in peace. Still another, joy. What an abundant harvest there will be when all God's children have the soil of faith enriched with my Word and Supper, and watered with my promises in Baptism.

JOHN: In all of this, Jesus, you have said nothing of God's law. What of the commandments, "Honor thy father and thy mother," and "Thou shalt not kill," and "Thou shalt not commit adultery," and all the others? Isn't obeying the law also bearing fruit?

JESUS: All that the law teaches is good. But no one can obey it apart from being a branch on the vine. Obedience that is only outward is not the harvest that pleases God. Rather, it is the fruit that comes by faith in me that the Father seeks.

JOHN: Then it is not enough to be religious and moral? What about the decent man in the community who has no faith or perhaps follows another god?

JESUS: Bearing fruit has nothing at all to do with being religious or moral. It has everything to do with being connected to me by faith. When you remain in the vine by faith, my Spirit is the life force that causes you to bear fruit. Apart from me there is no real fruit; there are just dead branches fit only to be cut off and burned.

JOHN: There are times, Jesus, when I know full well the fruit you want me to bear, but I don't. When I know I should love, I hate instead. What then? Will I be cut off?

JESUS: Only by unbelief can a branch be cut off. Even so, my Father can graft it back in by faith, giving it new life that it might still produce a crop for him. But that is not your concern. It is for you to remain in the vine by faith and grow strong through my word.

JOHN: What if I'm slow to bear fruit, or my branch is injured in one of the storms of life, then what?

JESUS: That is why all the branches grow on the same vine. The stronger branch with the big green leaves shades and protects the weaker branch struggling to grow. Together, the branches draw strength from the vine and support one another, each leaf and branch intertwined and lifting the others up. And thus, even the weak or injured branch bears fruit that pleases the Father.

JOHN: Then whether or not I bear fruit isn't a private matter, Jesus? It's the concern of all the others, too?

JESUS: There are many branches on the vine, none identical, and none independent. All grow together, drawing strength from the same root, producing a harvest of fruit that pleases God.

JOHN: Soon we'll be at the garden, Jesus. Shall we leave you here alone to pray as we've done before? Must this really be the last time?

JESUS: Yes, John. The enemy that would destroy the vine is approaching.

JOHN: Will he succeed, Jesus? If he does, the vine will never bear fruit for God and once again the vineyard will be abandoned.

JESUS: He will succeed, John. But in destroying the vine, the enemy will destroy himself. For though the vine dies, a shoot will spring up from the stump, bringing life to all who believe enabling them to bear abundant fruit. Do you believe this, John?

JOHN: Yes, Lord!

JESUS: Then don't be afraid. Your basket will be full. Stay here and watch while I pray.

Prayer

Lord of life, we thank you that though the vine was hewn down by the enemy, yet you have brought forth a living shoot, your Son, who was dead but who now lives. Through your word you have grafted us into him by faith that we might share in his life and grow abundant fruits of righteousness. Grant this to us, dear Father, for your glory. In Jesus' name. Amen.

Maundy Thursday
John 15:1-17

Children's Sermon

Item needed: a flowering branch from a fruit tree

Welcome, children! This is a very special week for Christians. Can anyone tell me what it's called? (*Perhaps a child will say, "Holy Week."*) Yes, it's Holy Week. Why do we call it Holy Week? (*Several may answer.*) That's right. This is the week in which Jesus died on the cross for our sins, and then rose from the dead on Easter Sunday.

Today is Maundy Thursday of Holy Week. Today we remember that Jesus gave us the Lord's Supper and taught us a new commandment, "Love one another." It was on Maundy Thursday that Jesus compared himself and his followers to a vine and its branches. "I am the True Vine and you are the branches," he said. The purpose of every branch in Jesus is to bear fruit.

I brought a branch from my peach tree to show you what Jesus means. Look at all the buds on this branch. They're all swelling up and just about to blossom. (*Pass the branch around.*) If the branch were on the tree, all these blossoms would become peaches. Are they going to become peaches now? (*Children will answer, "No!"*) You're right. When I cut the branch off the tree, it can't get nutrients and water from the tree trunk and the soil anymore. So the branch will die, won't it?

That's why Jesus says, "Remain in me." When you and I keep trusting Jesus and hear and believe God's word, we keep growing in our faith and produce spiritual fruit for him. We love God and our neighbor more and more and our lives are full of peace and joy. But if we stopped trusting Jesus and didn't hear and believe God's word anymore, we would dry up like a branch cut off from a fruit tree. There would be no fruit for Jesus.

Would you like to grow fruit in your life for Jesus? Good! So would I. Let's ask God to keep us trusting in Jesus and growing in faith so there will be lots of fruit in our lives for him.

Prayer

Dear Lord Jesus, thank you that you have made us branches on the Vine which is you. Through your word, help us always trust you as our Savior. Keep us growing in faith and love that we might produce a beautiful harvest of spiritual fruit for you. In your holy name we pray. Amen.

Good Friday
Isaiah 51:17-23
John 18:1-11 (12-27)

I Am He

MALCHUS: Jesus, I may never have a chance to speak with you again. And surely you have much on your mind, forced along as we are to the house of my master Caiaphas. You needn't speak to me if you'd rather not. I am, after all, the servant of your enemy.

JESUS: I don't mind, Malchus. Unless these soldiers say otherwise, I'd be happy to speak with you.

MALCHUS: Why did you do what you did back there in the Garden? None of it makes any sense. Especially that you would restore my ear, the one your disciple Peter cut off. Oh, don't misunderstand me. I'm grateful beyond words that you healed my ear. But why?

JESUS: What would you have done, Malchus, if one of your servants had cut off an enemy's ear?

MALCHUS: I would have drawn my sword and entered the fray, cutting off, not ears, but heads. If I had men to help me, we would have fought to the death. You wouldn't find me giving up without a fight.

JESUS: So an act of kindness disturbs you. Do you suppose that restoring a man's ear disturbs God?

MALCHUS: I hadn't looked at it that way. But there's so much more, Jesus, to what happened back there.

JESUS: Indeed there is, far more than you or even my disciples can comprehend.

MALCHUS: Why were you there in the first place? Surely you knew Judas was a traitor, that he would lead us right to you, given the opportunity. But you did nothing to evade the obvious. There you were, in the dark, isolated, vulnerable, just as Judas said we'd find you.

JESUS: Yes, I knew Judas and the others would come. They were on the march even while my disciples slept. But I had to be there. That is why my Father sent me. The hour had come for him to glorify me.

MALCHUS: By getting arrested? I know these people well, Jesus. You are going to be tried. They'll charge you with blasphemy, with treason, with whatever it takes to have you crucified. They've already made up their minds.

JESUS: The decision was rendered long before any of them were born.

MALCHUS: I'm not sure I understand, Jesus, but if I were you, I wouldn't have been there. And if I had been there, I would have lied about who I was or I would have run, just as your disciples ran, to save myself.

JESUS: And in doing so, you would have saved no one. I stayed and allowed myself to be arrested in order to save you, my enemy's slave, and indeed this whole mob of enemies, and my disciples too, all of whom have fled, trying to disassociate themselves from me.

MALCHUS: How would your staying save anyone? Just who are you anyway?

JESUS: Didn't you hear the words of those who came to arrest me? I asked them, "Who is it you want?" and they answered, "Jesus of Nazareth." I replied, "I am he."

MALCHUS: Yes, and you saw what happened. Never before have I seen soldiers and slaves and priests draw back and fall to the ground when a fugitive has been identified. But we all did. Something came over us, and we fell down. I have done that in the presence of my master when he threatened to whip me. But never have I seen grown men fall to the ground in the presence of a carpenter. Who are you, really, Jesus?

JESUS: As I said, I am he.

MALCHUS: Then I still don't know who you are.

JESUS: Oh, but you do! Malchus, you have lived with Caiaphas the priest for many years. Surely you have heard him read from the scrolls. Remember the words from Isaiah? "We all like sheep have gone astray, each of us has turned to his own way, and the Lord has laid on him the iniquity of us all." You have even observed that though I knew my enemies planned to kill me, I still waited in the garden for them to arrest me. Does not the prophet say, "He was led like a sheep to the slaughter, and as a sheep before her shearers is silent, so he did not open his mouth"? Does not all this tell you who I am?

MALCHUS: I am not a theologian, Jesus. I am a slave. I cut wood. I do laundry. I dress and feed my master. When he's angry, I feel the blows of his fist. I will never own a home or a shop. When I die, I'll be buried in an unmarked pit clothed with the only garment I own. Theology is a luxury I can't afford.

JESUS: But for those who know me, so much more is true: a soul that is free, a life with purpose, garments of righteousness, a mansion in heaven for a home.

MALCHUS: Who are you, Jesus?

JESUS: In the garden you learned who I am. I am the one whose word is always true. I am the one who can heal a severed ear with a touch. I am the one who causes the sword to be put away. I am one who loves even his enemies. I am the one who dies to save them from the slavery of their sin and guilt.

MALCHUS: The things you do sound more like a Messiah than a carpenter. Surely you are not the one who is to come?

JESUS: I am he.

MALCHUS: You, the Messiah? But I thought the Messiah would come with a glorious army and a powerful sword to destroy all that oppresses us. But your army is a pitiful band of disciples, one who turns traitor and others who sleep when danger threatens. And when one uses his sword, and that on an insignificant slave's ear, you make him put it away. You? You are the one we hoped for?

JESUS: I am he. My kingdom is not from this world and therefore it does not use the weapons of this world. My army is all who repent of sin and come to me in faith. My weapon is my word.

MALCHUS: Jesus, your army back there was sleeping. What sort of army is it that sleeps? And what can a word do?

JESUS: Mine is an army of the redeemed. Armed with only my word, my army can offer the forgiveness of sins. Do you know of any other army with such power? The Roman cohort? This temple guard of Caiaphas? What king do you know who restores a severed ear, gives sight to the blind, cleanses lepers or raises a widow's son to life?

MALCHUS: Even I have heard of these things. Everyone has talked about them. And my own relatives walking here with us have seen what you did to my ear. Yes, you must be the one! I must do something to stop the injustice that lies ahead! Jesus, I can help you escape! It's not too late! The same darkness that gave cover to this mob can hide you!

JESUS: So quickly you become like Peter, Malchus. There is nothing you can do. This is the plan of my Father. Shall I not drink the cup the Father has given me? It is because I drink this cup, that you will never have to drink it.

MALCHUS: No! I must do something!

JESUS: Don't you see, Malchus? Because of the cup I am about to drink, you need do nothing. It is all being done for you. Your sin, and the sin of this angry crowd, deserve the fullest measure of God's wrath. But I am about to take his wrath upon myself, in your place. It is for me to die, and be raised on the third day. It is for you to believe and have eternal life. Are you listening, Malchus? He who has ears to hear, let him hear!

MALCHUS: Thanks to you, Jesus, I do have ears, and I have heard. Our time together has been so short. Already we are at the house of Annas, and soon the house of Caiaphas. If there were only some other way.

JESUS: There is none. I am he.

MALCHUS: Yes, you are he. Good-bye, Jesus. Thank you, Jesus.

Prayer

Precious Savior, even in the midst of an angry crowd of enemies plotting your murder, still you are compassionate, restoring a man's ear, telling another to put up his sword. We confess that by our many sins and hardness of heart, we too have been numbered among your enemies. Forgive us and restore us. Heal our ears that we might hear of your love, and open our mouths that we might tell others of your salvation. Thank you for dying in our place. In your name we pray. Amen.

Good Friday
John 18:1-11

Children's Sermon

Item needed: a coffee cup and a cardboard sword

Hello, children! I saw several of you at church last night. Why are you here again? (*Someone will say, "Because it's Good Friday!"*) Yes, it's Good Friday. This is the day Jesus died. That makes us sad. If it makes us sad, what's "good" about it? (*Allow several to answer.*) That's right, we're sad Jesus died, but we're happy that he died to take away our sins. That's why it's called "Good Friday."

Jesus loves us so much, nothing would keep him from dying for our sins. When Jesus was arrested, one of his friends, Peter, pulled his sword and cut off a man's ear, like this! (*Pretend to do so with a volunteer.*) Do you remember what the man's name was? Yes, it was Malchus, the high priest's slave. Peter was ready to defend Jesus. He didn't want Jesus to die.

But Jesus made Peter put his sword away. (*Do it.*) Jesus healed Malchus. (*Pretend to be Jesus healing Malchus' ear.*) Then Jesus said, "Shall I not drink the cup the Father has given me?" Jesus meant that it was his job to do everything God had sent him here to do. God sent him to earth to die for our sins so that we could be forgiven and have a home in heaven.

Dying on the cross was like drinking a cup of terrible tasting medicine. Have you ever had to take terrible tasting medicine? It's no fun, is it? You might even cry. But your parents make you take it anyway. Why? (*Allow children to answer.*) Yes. Taking the medicine will help you get well. (*Pretend to drink from the cup.*)

That's why Jesus took the medicine of the cross. It was a terrible tasting cup, but because he drank it, you and I are saved from all our sins. Let's thank Jesus for what he did for us.

Prayer

Dear Jesus, it was for our sin that you died on the cross. You could have let Peter defend you. You could have said, "No," to the cross and walked away. But you didn't. Instead you loved us and died for us. You drank the cup God gave you and saved us. Thank you, Jesus. Amen.

Easter Sunday
Psalm 22
John 1:1-14, 8:12
Luke 24:13-35

I Am The Light Of The World

JESUS: I see you're going my way, toward Emmaus. Do you mind if I walk with you?

CLEOPAS: Actually, my friend and I were having a private conversation, but I suppose it's all right. It's really not safe to travel alone. My name is Cleopas, and you are ...?

JESUS: Just another neighbor. You look like you've had a distressing day. What's the trouble?

CLEOPAS: What's the trouble? Don't you know? Are you the only one who doesn't know the things that have happened these past three days in Jerusalem?

JESUS: What things?

CLEOPAS: Everything about Jesus of Nazareth, the one the priests and rulers turned over to Pilate to be crucified. It was just this past Friday that he died. How he once filled our hearts with joy and hope! We had hoped he would be the one to redeem Israel!

JESUS: You *had* hoped, but now you don't?

CLEOPAS: How can a dead man do anything? When he was with us, he seemed so different, his wonderful deeds; the things he said about himself: I am the Bread of Life, I am the Gate, I am the Good Shepherd, I am the Resurrection and the Life, I am the Way, the

Truth, and the Life, and I am the Light of the World. All these things he said to describe himself, and you know, I almost believed in him.

JESUS: But now you don't?

CLEOPAS: Like I said, he's dead.

JESUS: What makes you so sure?

CLEOPAS: I saw it all with my own eyes. I was there every step of the way up Golgotha. I heard the hammer blows as the soldiers drove the nails into his hands and feet. I listened to every word he said from the cross, even those impossible words, "Forgive them, for they know not what they do." Forgive them? For that cruelty? For that injustice? Maybe he wasn't who I hoped he would be, but he did nothing to deserve the cross. He died quickly, though. There was no need to break his legs, as they did to the others. But just to make sure, one of the soldiers thrust his spear into Jesus' side. He was dead, all right.

JESUS: So now your world is in darkness. Rather than joy and hope, your world is filled with sorrow and disappointment. You feel Jesus has failed you. He's not who he said he was. And so today you despair. The light he promised isn't shining for you anymore.

CLEOPAS: Yes, that's what I'm feeling.

JESUS: And you have no reason to change your mind?

CLEOPAS: No reasons of any importance. Oh, I suppose you should know that some of our women visited Jesus' tomb this morning as the sun was coming up. They said it was empty. They said there were angels there, ablaze with light, dressed in the whitest of garments. The angels had a message, "You're seeking the body of Jesus. He is not here. He has risen, just as he said."

JESUS: You didn't believe the women?

CLEOPAS: Well, you know how some women can be — emotional, gullible. Besides what can you see when the sun's just barely coming up? I think they probably wanted Jesus to be alive so much they just convinced themselves. But they surely seemed happy! And so excited! They ran all the way to the Upper Room to tell Peter and the others their story!

JESUS: What if it were true? Would that explain their joy and excitement?

CLEOPAS: Oh, sure, but that's impossible. The dead don't rise.

JESUS: Just how well did you know Jesus?

CLEOPAS: As well as anybody. I was there through most of his ministry.

JESUS: Were you there when the woman taken in adultery was brought to Jesus? He told her accusers that whoever was without sin should cast the first stone. They all left. Then he said to the woman, "Neither do I condemn you. Go and leave your life of sin." What kind of person would speak such words to a sinner, words of forgiveness? And do you remember what he said a little later to his disciples?

CLEOPAS: Yes, he said, "I am the Light of the World." He surely shined some light on the whole matter of sin and guilt. He made us see that we were all sinners who needed forgiveness.

JESUS: And right after that, he restored the sight of the man born blind. All that the Pharisees could see was that Jesus healed a blind man on the Sabbath. But the blind man could see far more; he could see that Jesus was from God.

CLEOPAS: Jesus was certainly light to that blind man, that's for sure. What a contrast his faith was to the darkness of unbelief in the hearts of the Pharisees.

JESUS: Cleopas, you have said it was impossible for the dead to be raised, yet you saw Jesus give sight to a blind man, something that has never before happened in the history of the world. Why is one more impossible than the other?

CLEOPAS: I never thought of that.

JESUS: And what about Lazarus, Jesus' friend whom he called out of the tomb alive after he had been dead for four days? Surely you heard about that!

CLEOPAS: Indeed I did! It was the talk of all Jerusalem and Judea!

JESUS: Isn't it interesting that even the religious leaders didn't question that miracle. They knew it happened. But they plotted against Jesus anyway because he was a threat to their power.

CLEOPAS: I'm beginning to understand. Maybe the story the women told was true after all. Could it be that Jesus is everything he said he was? Maybe he is the Light of the World! But that couldn't be. He's dead. Say, how do you know so much about Jesus?

JESUS: How slow you are to believe, Cleopas. Didn't the prophets speak of how the Christ would suffer and then enter glory? Aren't even the very details of his death foretold in the Psalms, even his words from the cross? And wasn't it Isaiah who said that the Christ would be the Lamb upon whom all the sins of the world would be laid and through whom all would be healed? Doesn't this shed light on the events of the last three days, Cleopas?

CLEOPAS: How blind I've been! The miles have gone by so quickly. Here's my house. Within my heart the light of hope is beginning to shine again. But out here in the street it will soon be dark. Won't you come in and eat with us?

JESUS: Your hospitality is appreciated and accepted. I would love to break bread at your table.

CLEOPAS: Here, I'll get the door. Dear wife! Meet my new friend, who's name I still don't know but who seems to know much about Jesus. Perhaps he would bless our meal for us? Friend, sit here in the best place. Here's the bread. Won't you offer a prayer?

JESUS: Indeed I will. Father, bless this bread to the nourishment of our bodies and bless also the hands that prepared it. Grant this household to know him who is the Light of the World.

CLEOPAS: Why, I know you! You're no stranger! You're Jesus! What the women said is true! They didn't make it up after all! You're alive! You, you ... Jesus? Where did you go? You were just here and now you've gone. Dear wife, I must go back to Jerusalem at once and tell the others! I've seen him, Jesus himself! He *is* alive! This bread is the very bread he broke! He lives! He lives! It's true, the Lord has risen!

Prayer
God of light and glory, illumine our hearts with him who is the light of the world. Help us to know that even now he lives to give us hope and forgiveness and eternal life. And grant us joyful boldness to proclaim to the world his victory over sin and death. In the name of our risen Savior, Jesus Christ, we pray. Amen.

Easter Sunday
John 8:12

Children's Sermon

Item needed: a small table lamp

Good morning, children. What a happy looking group! Why are you smiling? (*Most will answer, "Because it's Easter!"*) Yes, today is Easter, the day Jesus rose from the dead. Were some of you here on Good Friday? If you were, how did the church look inside? (*Allow several to answer.*) Yes, everything was very dark. There were no banners, no altar coverings, no beautiful flowers. Only one candle was left burning. It was a sad day because we were remembering that Jesus died.

But today is different. Everything is bright in the church. There are flowers everywhere. Look at all the candles! Each of you has your best clothes on, and you're smiling. Why? Because we're celebrating! Jesus isn't dead anymore. He's alive!

When I was little, I used to be afraid of the dark. I would lie in my bed and think the shadows on the wall were monsters. I would look at my clothes on the chair and think they were moving. Sometimes I'd would jump out of bed and go to my parents' bedroom and tell them I was afraid.

What do you think they would do? (*Let the children answer.*) Yes. Mom or Dad would take me back to my room, and turn on the light like this. (*Do it.*) We'd look all around the room together. I would see that there weren't any monsters and nothing was really moving. Then I'd get back in bed and happily go to sleep. (*Turn off light.*)

It was something like that for Jesus' friends when he died. Life had become very dark and scary. Even the sun stopped shining for a while. The disciples of Jesus were so frightened they locked themselves in a room.

Fortunately, some brave women went to Jesus' tomb very early in the morning on Easter Sunday to finish preparing him for burial. It was just barely daylight. Guess what they saw at the grave of Jesus! The tomb was open! There were angels as bright as lightning! And they said, "He is not here; he has risen!"

Would you have been afraid if you were there? So would I. But what the angels said was like a light coming on in the darkness. (*Turn on the lamp.*) Since Jesus is alive, we don't need to be afraid, ever! He's always with us protecting us from the real monsters of sin and death and the devil. Jesus said, "I am the Light of the World. Whoever follows me will never walk in darkness, but will have the light of life."

Because Jesus is alive, the light is always on in our life. Happy Easter!

Prayer
Dear Father in heaven, thank you that because Jesus lives we have no need to be afraid. The monsters of sin and death and the devil are defeated at the cross and the empty tomb. We are safe in Jesus who is the Light of the World. In his name we pray. Amen.